Table of Contents

What Is BMX?

The sport of BMX takes biking to the **extreme**. BMX stands for bicycle motocross. Motocross is a type of motorcycle racing that takes place on dirt tracks. In the early 1970s, people started riding bicycles on the tracks. They also began doing different tricks and flips.

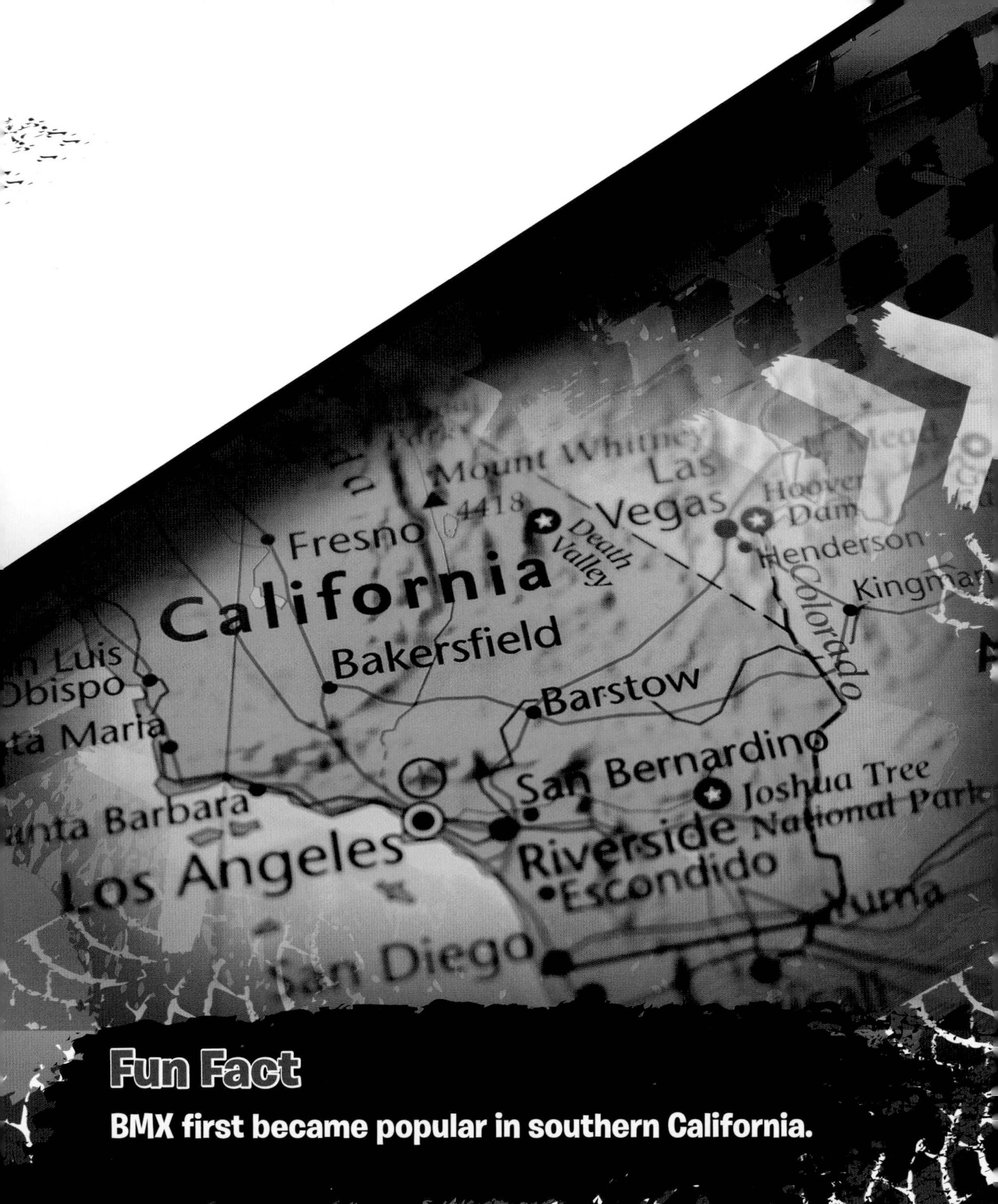

Fun Fact

BMX first became popular in southern California.

BMX in Action

BMX is one of the most popular extreme sports in the world. The two main forms of BMX are racing and **freestyle**. BMX racing is done on dirt or **paved** pathways or tracks. These tracks are made to be difficult, and can include jumps, sharp turns, and hills.

Fun Fact

BMX tracks are at least 1,000 feet (305 m) long. That's about the same size as the height of the Eiffel Tower!

In BMX freestyle, riders do stunts and tricks. There are different types of BMX freestyle.

Fun Fact

BMX Freestyle is now a part of the Summer Olympics.

In street freestyle, riders use public spaces to do tricks. This can include stairs, ledges, and railings.

Park is a type of freestyle where riders use **skate parks** to do different tricks. In the freestyle known as vert, **competitors** use a **ramp** called a half-pipe to do jumps. They usually perform tricks in the air with each jump.

Flatland is another type of freestyle. Competitors use smooth, flat surfaces to do spins while balancing on their bikes. In the freestyle known as trails, or dirt jumping, riders jump off dirt mounds and do midair tricks.

Fun Fact

Flatland was created by R.L. Osborn, Bob Haro, and Bob Morales.

Parts of a BMX Bike

The parts used to create a BMX bike play a very important role in this extreme sport. The **frame** is the biggest part of the bike. The way the frame is created, including the type of material used and the size of the tubes, will make one bike feel different from another.

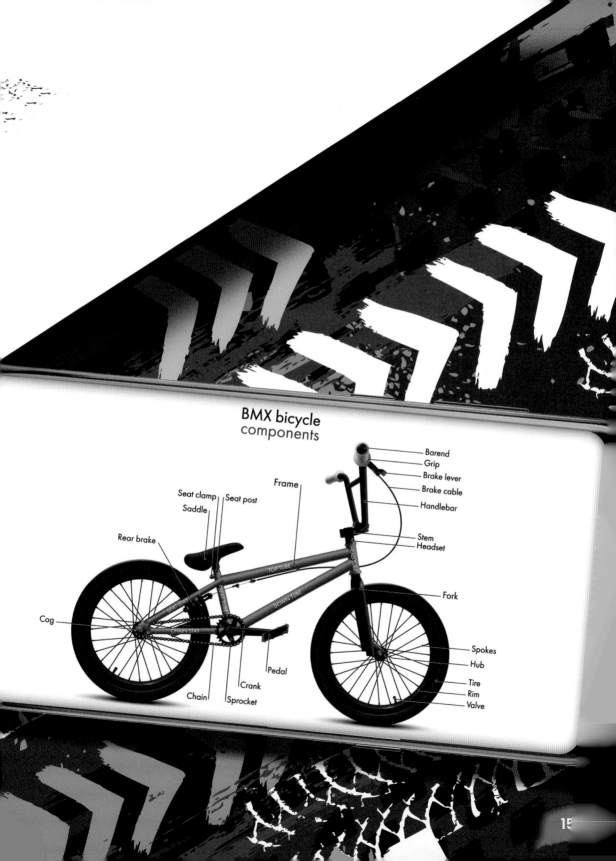

BMX bicycle
components

Barend
Grip
Brake lever
Brake cable
Handlebar

Frame

Seat clamp Seat post

Saddle

Stem
Headset

Rear brake

Fork

TOP TUBE

HEAD TUBE

SEAT STAY

DOWN TUBE

SEAT TUBE

Cog

CHAIN STAY

Spokes
Hub

Tire
Rim
Valve

Pedal

Crank

Chain   Sprocket

The handlebars of a BMX bike help with the performance of different types of tricks. They also help the rider have better control of the bike. The BMX fork helps with steering and front-wheel tricks.

Fun Fact

BMX bikes go up to 35 miles per hour (56 km/h).

The wheels are also an important part of a BMX bike. The type of wheels depends on if the bike is being used for BMX racing or freestyle.

Your BMX Career

Still trying to decide if you're ready to start riding BMX? If you have a local BMX club nearby, drop in for a visit and try out some bikes. Or find a BMX coach who can teach you some BMX basics.

Fun Fact

Sports in the X Games include BMX, skateboarding, skiing, and snowboarding.

If you become a good BMX rider you might be able to compete in the X Games or other **tournaments**. The X Games is an extreme sports event held twice a year, in the winter and the summer.

BMX Legends

Throughout the history of BMX there have been many different **legends**. One of them is Mat Hoffman. Hoffman was born on January 9, 1972. At the age of 17, he became the youngest rider in BMX history to turn **professional**. Hoffman does BMX vert.

Fun Fact

In 1989, Hoffman did the first 900 air on a BMX bike. That's a spin of two-and-a-half turns in the air!

Ryan Nyquist is another BMX legend. Born on March 6, 1979, he has won 16 X Games medals. Nyquist participates in freestyle events and is the best in BMX park and dirt jumping. He has made 60 Dew Tour finals appearances, the record for the most of all time.

Fun Fact

Nyquist was born in Los Gatos, California.

Hannah Roberts is a three-time world champion BMX rider. Roberts was born on August 10, 2001. She won her first world championship at the age of 16. Roberts won a silver medal in BMX Freestyle at the 2020 Summer Olympic Games in Tokyo.

Charlotte Worthington is another legend in BMX. Worthington was born on June 26, 1996. She won a gold medal for BMX Freestyle at the 2020 Olympics in Tokyo. Worthington is the only female to land a 360-degree backflip in BMX competition history.

Fun Fact

Worthington was a chef at a Mexican restaurant for three years before participating in the Olympics.

Glossary

competitor (kuhm·PEH·tuh·ter): Someone who is trying to win or do better than others

extreme (ek·STREEM): Something that is far beyond the normal

frame (FRAME): The structure or shape of something

freestyle (FREE·stile): In sports, a performance or competition in which participants are allowed to use different styles or methods

legend (LEH·jind): Someone who is famous and admired for doing something well

paved (PAYVD): Something that is covered with a material, such as concrete or asphalt, to make a hard, smooth surface

professional (pruh· FEH·shuh·nuhl): Someone who is paid to participate in a sport or activity

ramp (RAMP): A piece of equipment with a slope

skate park (SKEHYT pahrk): An outdoor space with structures and surfaces for skateboarding

tournament (TUR·nuh·ment): A competition with many participants

Index

Websites to Visit

www.xgames.com

www.usabmx.com

http://learnbmxracing.com

About the Author

Bernard Conaghan lives in South Carolina with his German shepherd named Duke. Every year he goes snowboarding in Switzerland. He is a coach on his son's football team. He always eats one scoop of peach ice cream after dinner.

Written by: Bernard Conaghan
Designed by: Jen Bowers
Series Development: James Earley
Proofreader: Melissa Boyce
Educational Consultant: Marie Lemke M.Ed.

Photographs: Cover image ©2016 MarcelClemens/Shutterstock, background ©Matisson_ART/Shutterstock; p.3 ©2017 Konstantin Tronin/Shutterstock; p.4 ©2019 homydesign/Shutterstock; p.5 ©2017 Alexander Lukatskiy/Shutterstock; p.6 ©2014 Eric Buermeyer/Shutterstock; p.7 ©2013 LiliGraphie/Shutterstock; p.8 ©2021 roibu/Shutterstock; p.9 ©2020 Mihail Fedorenko/Shutterstock0; p.11 ©2017 Rocksweeper/Shutterstock; p.13 ©2014 smileimage9/Shutterstock; p.14 & 15 ©Farber/Shutterstock, phone ©2017 Vasin Lee/Shutterstock; p.16 ©Farber/Shutterstock, ©2018 Evgeniy Marin/Shutterstock; p.17 ©Farber/Shutterstock; p.18 ©2018 Burdun Iliya/Shutterstock; p.19 ©2016 Eric Buermeyer/Shutterstock; p.20 ©2011 Juan Camilo Bernal/Shutterstock, medals © Net Vector/Shutterstock; p.22 ©2015 Tinseltown/Shutterstock; p.25 ©2009 Haslam Photography/Shutterstock; p.26 ©Leo Zhukov/Sporty Photographer/CC BY-SA 4.0/https://en.wikipedia.org/wiki/Hannah_Roberts; p.27 ©2021 fifg/Shutterstock; p.28 ©National Lottery Good Causes/CC BY 3.0/https://en.wikipedia.org/wiki, ©2021 fifg/Shutterstock; p.29 ©2020 StreetVJ/Shutterstock, ©2019 Tatiana Bralnina/Shutterstock

Crabtree Publishing

crabtreebooks.com   800-387-7650

Printed in the U.S.A./012023/CG20220815

Published in Canada
Crabtree Publishing
616 Welland Avenue
St. Catharines, Ontario
L2M 5V6

Published in the United States
Crabtree Publishing
347 Fifth Avenue
Suite 1402-145
New York, New York 10016

Library and Archives Canada Cataloguing in Publication
Available at Library and Archives Canada

Library of Congress Cataloging-in-Publication Data
Available at the Library of Congress

Hardcover: 978-1-0396-9662-4
Paperback: 978-1-0396-9769-0
Ebook (pdf): 978-1-0396-9983-0
Epub: 978-1-0396-9876-5